# INFOGRAPHIC TOP 10s

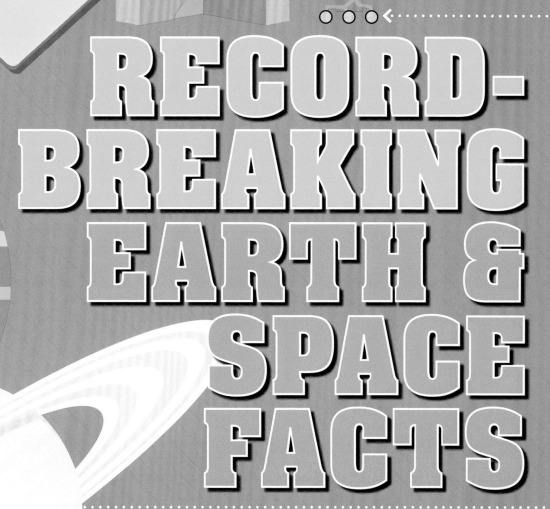

# RECORD-BREAKING EARTH & SPACE FACTS

Jon Richards and Ed Simkins

HUNGRY TOMATO™

MINNEAPOLIS

# CONTENTS

**pages 4–5**
See what is inside a volcano and discover how violent a volcanic eruption can be.

**pages 10–11**
Discover why conditions on our planet are just right for life to exist.

# WELCOME!

From the biggest to the closest and from the driest to the fastest, this book looks at the amazing record-breakers in the universe. It uses stunning icons, graphics, and visualizations to show you how these amazing planets, stars, comets, and asteroids are true galactic greats.

**pages 22–23**
Find out about the planets that exist outside the solar system and measure how big they are.

**pages 26–27**
Discover how much moon rock was brought back by the Apollo missions.

# CRACKED SURFACE

‹ ⋯⋯⋯⋯⋯⋯⋯⋯ ›

The surface of Earth is cracked like the shell of an egg into various, uneven, and jagged tectonic plates. These move around slowly, bashing into each other and creating shattering earthquakes, spouting volcanoes, and towering mountains.

## What's inside a volcano

A volcano is an opening in the crust where molten rock, ash, steam, and gases escape from the planet's interior.

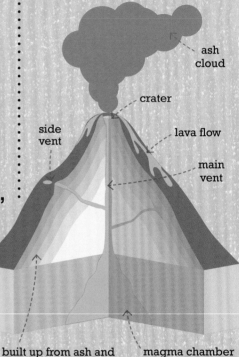

ash cloud

crater

side vent

lava flow

main vent

cone built up from ash and lava from previous eruptions

magma chamber

## Most active volcano

The most active volcano on the planet is **Kilauea in Hawaii**. It has been erupting continuously since 1983, and lava erupts from it at a rate of 177 cubic feet (5 cubic meters) every second.

**8 mins. 20 secs.**

That's fast enough to fill an Olympic swimming pool in...

Lava reaches 2,282°F (1,250°C)—hot enough to melt gold.

Pyroclastic flows are clouds of scorching rock and gas that pour out of a volcano. They typically move at speeds of 50 miles (80 kilometers) per hour, but the fastest can travel at **298 miles (480 km) per hour**, which is **1.5 times faster** than a Formula One car.

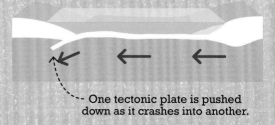

## How mountains are formed

**Mount Everest** is the tallest mountain on Earth and is **29,029 feet (8,848 m)** high. It was created by two tectonic plates crashing into each other, forming the towering **Himalaya**.

One tectonic plate is pushed down as it crashes into another.

**90 percent**

of volcanoes are
found around the
Pacific Ring of Fire.

Volcanoes can
send an ash cloud
up to an altitude of
19 miles (30 km).

That's 3.5 times the
height of Mount
Everest.

# LARGEST TECTONIC PLATES

| | | |
|---|---|---|
| 1. | **Pacific**—39.9 million square miles (103.3 million sq. km) | |
| 2. | North American—29.3 million square miles (75.9 million sq. km) | |
| 3. | **Eurasian**—26.2 million square miles (67.8 million sq. km) | |
| 4. | African—23.7 million  square miles (61.3 million sq. km) | |
| 5. | **Antarctic**—23.5 million square miles (60.9 million sq. km) | |
| 6. | Australian—18.1 million square miles (47 million sq. km) | |
| 7. | **South American**—16.8 million square miles (43.6 million sq. km) | |
| 8. | Somalia—6.45 million square miles (16.7 million sq. km) | |
| 9. | **Nazca**—6 million square miles (15.6 million sq. km) | |
| 10. | Indian—4.6 million square miles (11.9 million sq. km) | |

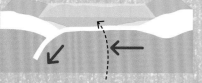

As the plates move together, the rock
between them starts to clump up.

Rock is pushed up between the
plates, creating mountains.

# Growing Himalaya

The Himalaya are currently growing
at a rate of about 0.4 inches
(1 centimeter) per year.

5

# DRY PLANET

‹ ···················· ›

Deserts are the driest places on the planet, receiving less than 10 inches (25 cm) of precipitation a year. They cover about one-third of the world's land and range in habitat from the scorching wastes of the Sahara in Africa to the frozen realm of Antarctica.

## Ice desert

**Antarctica** is the largest desert in the world (bigger than the continental United States). It is actually covered with water, but that is all **frozen**.

The **average thickness** of the ice is more than 1 mile (1.6 km). That's twice the height of the **Burj Khalifa**, the world's tallest building.

## Atacama Desert

The **Atacama Desert** in Chile is a rain shadow desert and the driest place on the planet. Its average rainfall is just 0.004 inches (0.1 millimeters) per year—that's just **0.4 inches (1 cm) of rain every 100 years.**

If the ice caps melted, the sea level would rise **197 feet (60 m)**

■ Flooded

...and the world's coastlines would look like this.

The **hottest** and **coldest** temperatures recorded on Earth were both measured in **deserts**.

| -128.6°F (-89.2°C) | -0.4°F (-18°C) | 9.9°F (-12.3°C) | 32°F (0°C) | 59°F (15°C) | 98.6°F (37°C) | 134.1°F (56.7°C) |
|---|---|---|---|---|---|---|
| **Vostok Station, Antarctica** | Optimum temperature for a freezer | Highest temperature recorded at the South Pole | Freezing point of water | Average temperature of Earth | Body temperature | **Furnace Creek, Death Valley, California** |

❄ Lowest

 Highest

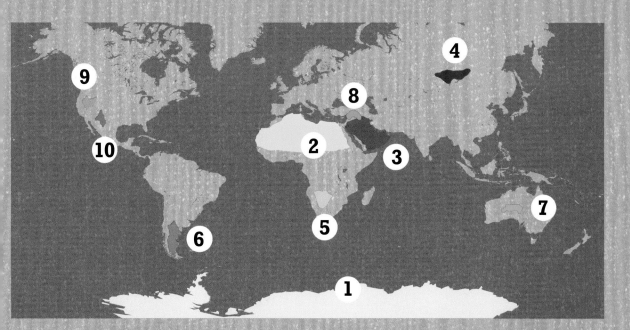

# LARGEST DESERTS IN THE WORLD

1. **Antarctic—5.5 million square miles (14.2 million sq. km)**

2. Sahara—3.3 million square miles (8.6 million sq. km)

3. **Arabian Desert—900,000 square miles (2.3 million sq. km)**

4. Gobi Desert—500,000 square miles (1.3 million sq. km)

5. **Kalahari Desert—360,000 square miles (930,000 sq. km)**

6. Patagonian Desert—260,000 square miles (673,000 sq. km)

7. **Great Victoria Desert—250,000 square miles (647,000 sq. km)**

8. Syrian Desert—200,000 square miles (518,000 sq. km)

9. **Great Basin Desert—190,000 square miles (492,000 sq. km)**

10. Chihuahuan Desert—109,000 square miles (282,000 sq. km)

## How a rain shadow desert forms

rain

wind

dry air

evaporation

mountain

**Water vapor** is picked up from the ocean to create moist air. This air is pushed up by a mountain range, where the water falls as rain. This leaves **dry air** to pass over to the other side of the mountains, creating the very dry conditions that form rain shadow deserts.

# LIFE ON EARTH

Earth is the only place in the solar system where life has been found (so far). It is the perfect distance from the sun to be the right temperature for liquid water, which is vital for life to exist.

**1**

The **forested area** of Russia is about the same size as the **entire country** of Brazil.

**2**

**3**

**4**

A single tree can absorb about 49 pounds (22 kilograms) of carbon dioxide in a year and produce enough oxygen for two people.

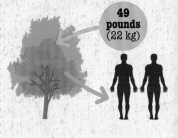

49 pounds (22 kg)

1.85 pounds (0.84 kg)

An average adult uses about 1.85 pounds (0.84 kg) of oxygen every day.

2 pounds (1 kg)

The average person exhales just over 2 pounds (1 kg) of carbon dioxide every day.

# COUNTRIES WITH THE LARGEST COMBINED FOREST AREA

1. **Russia—3.3 million square miles (8.5 million sq. km)**

2. Brazil—2.1 million square miles (5.4 million sq. km)

3. **Canada—930,000 square miles (2.4 million sq. km)**

4. United States—890,000 square miles (2.3 million sq. km)

5. **China—620,000 square miles (1.6 million sq. km)**

6. Australia—580,000 square miles (1.5 million sq. km)

7. **Democratic Republic of the Congo—540,000 square miles (1.4 million sq. km)**

8. Indonesia—390,000 square miles (1 million sq. km)

9. **Angola—269,000 square miles (698,000 sq. km)**

10. Peru—252,000 square miles (652,000 sq. km)

## Biomass facts

The combined mass of living things is called biomass. These figures show the creatures with some of the greatest biomass.

**Humans**
**386 million tons**
(350 million metric tons)
Seven billion people weighing an average of 110 pounds (50 kg) each.

**Termites**
**491 million tons**
(445 million metric tons)
A single termite nest can be home to millions of individual termites.

**Atlantic krill**
**418 million tons**
(379 million metric tons)
Trillions of these tiny creatures swarm together providing food for other marine animals.

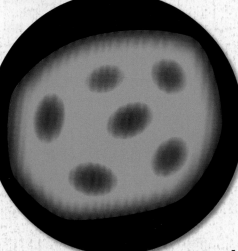

**Cows**
**717 million tons**
(650 million metric tons)
There are only 1.3 billion cows in the world, but they weigh 1,100 pounds (500 kg) each, making their total biomass nearly twice that of humans.

**Cyanobacteria**
**1.1 billion tons**
(1 billion metric tons)
Some of the smallest living things on the planet make up the greatest amount of biomass.

**Blue whales ◓**
**550,000 tons**
(500,000 metric tons)
In contrast, the total biomass of the largest animal to have ever lived is just 550,000 tons.

# THE SOLAR SYSTEM

<‹ ·········································· ›>

The family of planets, dwarf planets, and small objects, such as asteroids, is called the solar system. At its center is a ball of burning gas: the sun. So what are the largest objects in the solar system in diameter?

## 6 Earth
Earth is the third planet from the sun, and it has one natural satellite: the moon.

### 7,918 miles (12,742 km)

## 7 Venus
The second planet from the sun has an atmosphere that's so thick that we cannot see the planet's surface.

### 7,521 miles (12,104 km)

## 8 Mars
Mars is called the red planet because its surface contains a lot of iron oxide, or rust.

### 4,213 miles (6,780 km)

## 9 Ganymede
Orbiting Jupiter, Ganymede is the largest moon in the solar system and bigger than the planet Mercury.

### 3,273 miles (5,268 km)

## 10 Titan
Titan is Saturn's largest moon, and its surface has seas, lakes, and rivers of methane and ethane.

### 3,201 miles (5,152 km)

## Giant planet

Jupiter has about 1,320 times the volume of Earth. Jupiter's **diameter** is 11 times that of Earth, and Jupiter has a surface area that is 120 times **bigger**

However, it is only 317 times Earth's mass, because its **density** is one-quarter that of our planet.

## Goldilocks zone

If a planet is too close to the sun, then conditions are **too hot** for life to exist. If a planet is too far away, conditions are **too cold**. In between is a region called the Goldilocks zone, where conditions are **just right** for life.

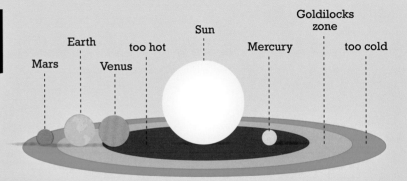

Mars — Earth — Venus — too hot — Sun — Mercury — Goldilocks zone — too cold

## 4 Uranus

This planet is a bright blue color because its atmosphere contains a lot of methane.

**31,518 miles
(50,724 km)**

## 5 Neptune

This planet is almost the same size as Uranus, and it takes nearly 165 years to orbit the sun.

**30,599 miles
(49,244 km)**

## 3 Saturn

Saturn is surrounded by a bright ring system, which is made up of pieces of ice and rock.

**72,367 miles
(116,464 km)**

## 2 Jupiter

The largest planet in the solar system, Jupiter is the fifth planet from the sun.

**88,846 miles (142,984 km)**

## 1 Sun

The sun produces light and heat by fusing together hydrogen atoms, which releases energy.

**864,337 miles
(1,391,016 km)**

## Sun facts

**It makes up 99.8 percent of the entire solar system's mass.**
It will continue to shine for 5.5 billion years, before expanding beyond Earth's orbit and then shrinking to form a tiny white dwarf star.

# IN A SPIN

Every planet spins around on its axis, creating periods of day and night. Jupiter is the fastest-spinning planet in the solar system, and its day only lasts for 9.8 Earth hours.

## PLANETS AND DWARF PLANETS WITH THE LONGEST DAYS (EARTH TIME)

1. **Venus—245 days, 0 hours, 25 minutes, 55 seconds**
2. Mercury—58 days, 15 hours, 30 minutes, 14 seconds
3. **Sun—25 days, 9 hours, 7 minutes, 26 seconds**
4. Pluto—6 days, 9 hours, 17 minutes, 17 seconds
5. **Eris—1 day, 1 hour, 53 minutes, 46 seconds**
6. Mars—24 hours, 37 minutes, 26 seconds
7. **Earth—23 hours, 56 minutes, 41 seconds**
8. Makemake—22 hours, 29 minutes, 17 seconds
9. **Uranus—17 hours, 13 minutes, 55 seconds**
10. Neptune—16 hours, 6 minutes, 4 seconds

## Lengths of the seasons

The planets move around the sun in paths called **orbits**. Because the planets are **tilted**, different parts of each planet point toward the sun at different parts of these orbits, creating the **seasons**. The length of the planets' seasons varies greatly depending on their **tilt** and the **length** of their orbit.

**Mars** 7 months

**Earth** 90–93 days

**Venus** 55–58 days

**Jupiter** 3 years

**Saturn** 7 years

**Uranus** 20 years

## Changing shape

Jupiter's fast spin actually **squashes** the planet slightly, creating a shape called an oblate spheroid. Jupiter is more than **2,800 miles (4,500 km) wider** than it is **tall**.

**85,965 miles** (138,347 km)

**88,846 miles** (142,984 km)

## Axial tilt

The objects that make up the solar system spin around at different angles, known as the **axial tilt**. The images here show the planets in the solar system with the greatest axial tilt.

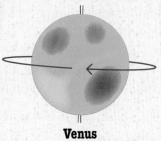

**Venus**
**177.3°**

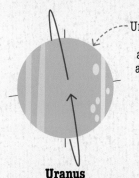

Uranus has its axis at an angle of 98° and spins on its side.

**Uranus**

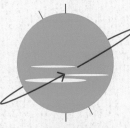

**Neptune**
**28.32°**

**Saturn**
**26.7°**

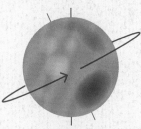

**Mars**
**25°**

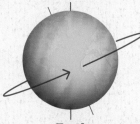

**Earth**
**23.5°**

**Jupiter**
**3.13°**

## Venus

The planet Venus actually spins in the **opposite direction** to the other planets—this is known as **retrograde rotation**. If Earth rotated in the same direction as Venus, then the sun would rise in the west and set in the east.

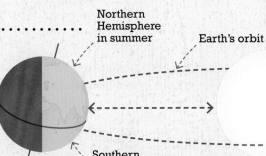

Northern Hemisphere in summer

Earth's orbit

Southern Hemisphere in winter

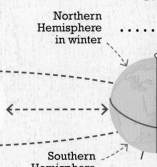

Northern Hemisphere in winter

Southern Hemisphere in summer

Neptune 40 years

# ON THE SURFACE

The four planets closest to the sun have rocky surfaces that are covered with towering peaks, huge chasms, and the scars of impacts from asteroids and comets.

This Martian volcano is the same size as Arizona.

Arizona

Its peak is **three times** higher than Mount Everest.

The six craters (calderas) at the summit are about 53 miles (85 km) wide—nearly twice the size of Greater London, United Kingdom, which is 30 miles (48 km) wide.

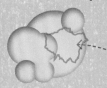

Greater London

six craters

## Valles Marineris

This huge canyon on Mars is up to 6 miles (10 km) deep. That's about 10 times the depth of the Grand Canyon.

It stretches around 20 percent of **Mars** and would stretch across **North America**.

② ④ ⑥ ⑦

The huge peak of Pavonis Mons on Mars measures 233 miles (375 km) across.

10

When measured from the sea floor, Mauna Kea is the tallest mountain on Earth. It is one of five volcanoes that make up Hawaii.

# TALLEST MOUNTAINS IN THE SOLAR SYSTEM (HEIGHT)

1. **Olympus Mons (Mars)—15.4 miles (24.8 km)**

2. Rheasilvia (Vesta)—13.1 miles (21.1 km)

3. **Equatorial ridge (Iapetus)—12.3 miles (19.8 km)**

4. Ascraeus Mons (Mars)—11.2 miles (18.1 km)

5. **Boosaule Montes (Io)—10.8 miles (17.4 km)**

6. Arsia Mons (Mars)—9.8 miles (15.8 km)

7. **Pavonis Mons (Mars)—8.6 miles (13.9 km)**

8. Elysium Mons (Mars)—7.7 miles (12.5 km)

9. **Maxwell Montes (Venus)—6.7 miles (10.9 km)**

10. Mauna Kea (Earth)—5.7 miles (9.1 km)

A 62-mile-wide (100 km) asteroid hit Mercury about four billion years ago, creating a huge crater called the Caloris basin. This is 963 miles (1,550 km) wide and could contain the state of Texas.

**1** Olympus Mons is surrounded by a cliff that is about 6 miles (10 km) high.

Boosaule Montes is found on Jupiter's moon, Io, the most volcanically active body in the solar system.

Maxwell Montes is a mountain range that is about 528 miles (850 km) long and 435 miles (700 km) wide.

# DEEP IMPACT

The solar system is not a safe place! Millions of pieces of rock and ice are flying around at enormous speeds. Sometimes they slam into planets with devastating results.

## Yucatán impact

About **66 million years ago,** an object about **6 miles (10 km)** across hit the Earth with the force of around **one billion atomic bombs**.

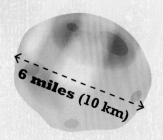

6 miles (10 km)

The object was traveling at a speed of nearly **19 miles (30 km) a second.** That's more than 150 times faster than a **jet airliner**.

Gulf of Mexico

crater

Yucatán Peninsula

Mexico

At the moment of impact, the asteroid created a **crater** that was **62 miles (100 km)** across and about **19 miles (30 km)** deep.

**62 miles (100 km)**

**19 miles (30 km)**

It's likely that the impact created an enormous **tsunami,** measuring **2.5 to 3 miles (4 to 5 km)** high—about 6.5 times the height of the **Burj Khalifa,** the tallest building in the world.

2.5 to 3 miles (4 to 5 km)

The collision threw up so much **dust and pollution** that scientists believe it blocked out the sun for up to **six months,** leading to...

...acid rain and...

...the collapse of photosynthesis...

...and a global temperature reduction.

This **change in conditions** was so great that it caused the **extinction** of the **dinosaurs**.

## Shoemaker-Levy 9

In 1994, fragments from the comet Shoemaker-Levy 9 slammed into Jupiter with incredible force. The pieces were traveling at 134,000 miles (216,000 km) per hour.

The largest piece was about **2 to 2.5 miles (3 to 4 km)** wide and left a hole in its atmosphere **twice the size of Earth**.

Earth

impact scars

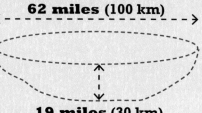

# BIGGEST CRATERS IN THE SOLAR SYSTEM (DIAMETER)

1. **Borealis basin (Mars)—5,300 miles (8,500 km)**
2. Valhalla (Callisto)—2,500 miles (4,000 km)
3. **South Pole-Aitken basin (moon)—1,555 miles (2,500 km)**
4. Hellas Planitia (Mars)—1,300 miles (2,100 km)
5. **Argyre Planitia (Mars)—1,100 miles (1,800 km)**
6. Caloris basin (Mercury)— 960 miles (1,550 km)
7. **Isidis Planitia (Mars)—930 miles (1,500 km)**
8. Asgard (Callisto)—870 miles (1,400 km)
9. **Mare Imbrium (moon)—684 miles (1,100 km)**
10. Turgis (Iapetus)—360 miles (580 km)

## How the moon was formed

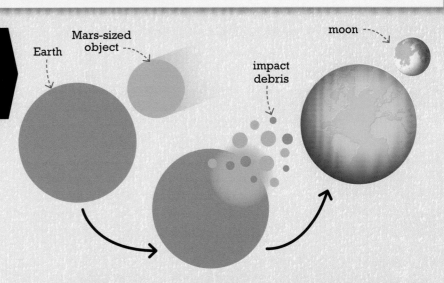

About 4.6 billion years ago, an object the size of **Mars** slammed into **Earth**, creating a spray of debris that clumped together to form the **moon**.

## Chelyabinsk meteor

In 2013, a **66-foot-wide (20 m)** piece of rock with a mass of **11,000 tons (10,000 metric tons)** entered Earth's atmosphere and exploded in the air over Russia. **The explosion injured 1,200 people.** It had a force equivalent to about **550,000 tons (500,000 metric tons)** of TNT—nearly **30 times** the force of the atomic bomb dropped on Hiroshima.

# SURFACE CONDITIONS

From scorching worlds to freezing globes, conditions on the solar system's planets and minor planets vary greatly. On some planets, the gravity is so great that you would struggle to move, while on others it is so small that you could leap unbelievably high.

Boiling point of mercury
**675°F (357°C)**

Melting point of lead
**621°F (327°C)**

| **842°F** (450°C) | **752°F** (400°C) | **662°F** (350°C) | **572°F** (300°C) | **482°F** (250°C) | **392°F** (200°C) | **302°F** (150°C) |
|---|---|---|---|---|---|---|

Boiling point of sulphur **833°F (445°C)**

## Venus

**1**

Venus's thick atmosphere is made up almost entirely of carbon dioxide. This acts like an enormous greenhouse, trapping heat and warming the planet to scorching temperatures.

## What would you weigh?

How the weight of a 165-pound (75 kg) person would vary on different bodies in the solar system.

| **Pluto** 11 pounds (5 kg) (×0.06) | **Moon** 27.3 pounds (12.4 kg) (×0.17) | **Mars** 62.2 pounds (28.2 kg) (×0.38) | **Mercury** 62.4 pounds (28.3 kg) (×0.38) | **Uranus** 146.8 pounds (66.6 kg) (×0.89) | **Venus** 150 pounds (68 kg) (×0.9) | **Earth** 165 pounds (75 kg) (×1) | **Saturn** 175.9 pounds (79.8 kg) (×1.06) | **Neptune** 185.8 pounds (84.3 kg) (×1.12) | **Jupiter** 390.9 pounds (177.3 kg) (×2.36) |

## Pluto

The gravity on Pluto, a dwarf planet, is only about 0.06 of that on Earth. A person who could make a 10-foot (3 m) slam dunk in basketball would be able to leap up to a height of 148 feet (45 m) on Pluto!

Highest temperature recorded on Earth **134.1°F (56.7°C)**

Freezing point of water

1. **Venus 864°F (462°C)**
2. Earth 59°F (15°C)
3. **Mars −81°F (−63°C)**
=3. **Mercury −81°F (−63°C)**
5. **Vesta −139.9°F (−95.5°C)**
6. **Ceres −157°F (−105°C)**
7. **Jupiter −229°F (−145°C)**
8. Saturn −283°F (−175°C)
9. **Neptune −360°F (−218°C)**
10. Uranus −371°F (−224°C)

| 122°F (50°C) | 32°F (0°C) | −58°F (−50°C) | −148°F (−100°C) | −238°F (−150°C) | −328°F (−200°C) | −418°F (−250°C) |

Human body temperature **98.6°F (37°C)**

**2**

**=3**

**=3**

**5**

**6**

**7**

**9**

**10**

**8**

## Mercury

The temperature on Mercury ranges from **842°F (450°C)** on the side facing the sun to **−274°F (−170°C)** on the side facing away from the sun. **That's a temperature range of 1,148°F (620°C)—the greatest in the solar system.**

842°F (450°C)

−274°F (−170°C)

19

# SMALL BODIES

Comets and asteroids may be small compared with the planets, but they can cause spectacular events, including glowing comet tails and shooting stars. The solar system is populated with millions of these small bodies.

The moon

①

②

③

④

⑤

⑥

⑦

⑧

⑧

⑩

## Dwarf planet

The largest object in the asteroid belt is called **Ceres**. It has a diameter of **590 miles (950 km)** and was first spotted in 1801. It was initially classified as an **asteroid**, but in 2006, it was reclassified as a **dwarf planet**. A dwarf planet is an object that **orbits** the sun, is **roughly** round in shape, and hasn't cleared its orbit of **other objects**.

On its own, Ceres accounts for 25 percent of the asteroid belt's total mass.

# LARGEST ASTEROIDS (DIAMETER)

1. 2 Pallas—339 miles (545 km)
2. 4 Vesta—329 miles (530 km)
3. 10 Hygiea—253 miles (407 km)
4. 511 Davida—203 miles (326 km)
5. 704 Interamnia—196 miles (316 km)
6. 52 Europa—188 miles (302 km)
7. 87 Sylvia—162 miles (260 km)
8. 31 Euphrosyne—158 miles (255 km)
=8. 15 Eunomia—158 miles (255 km)
10. 16 Psyche—157 miles (253 km)

**Most asteroids** are found in a zone between Mars and Jupiter known as the asteroid belt. Scientists believe that the belt has more than 750,000 asteroids that are larger than 0.6 miles (1 km) across.

## Comet lander

In November 2014, the lander **Philae** landed on the 2.5-mile-wide (4 km) comet 67P/Churyumov-Gerasimenko after a journey of **4 billion miles (6.4 billion km)**.

## Comet facts

Comet particles that are bigger than **0.04 inches (2 mm)** burn up at 2,912°F (1,600°C) as they enter the atmosphere, creating **shooting stars**.

**actual size**

2 mins.

Comet particles stream out at speeds of **217 miles (350 km)** a second. That is quick enough to travel around Earth in **less than two minutes**.

Every day, about 331 tons (300 metric tons) of dust, much of it from comets, reaches Earth—about the weight of **1.5 blue whales**.

In 2007, the tail of Comet McNaught was measured at more than **139 million miles (224 million km) long**.

## Comet tails

**That's about 1.5 times the distance from Earth to the sun.**

93,000,000 miles (149,600,000 km)

# DISTANT WORLDS

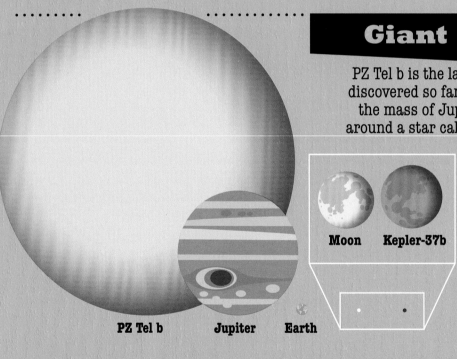

⟨‹ ···························· ›⟩

Until recently, no one had discovered planets outside the solar system. However, in the last 25 years, hundreds of these exoplanets have been found circling other stars, and some of these are the largest planets ever discovered.

**The exoplanet known as** Kepler-42 c completes an orbit around its star in just 4.3 hours.

## Giant planet

PZ Tel b is the largest **exoplanet** discovered so far. It has **36 times** the mass of Jupiter and orbits around a star called PZ Telescopii.

Moon    Kepler-37b

PZ Tel b        Jupiter        Earth

## Kepler-37b

One of the smallest known exoplanets is Kepler-37b. It is about the size of the moon, has a year that lasts just 13 days, and has a surface temperature of 797°F (425°C).

PZ Tel b orbits its star at 18 times the distance from the sun to Earth. Astronomers call this sun–Earth distance an **astronomical unit** (AU).

‹– – – – – – – – – – – – – – – 18 AU

‹– 1 AU

PZ Telescopii and its giant planet lie about **175 light-years** from Earth and can be seen in the constellation Telescopium.

Discovered in 2013, **Kepler-78b** is the same size as Earth, but it orbits its star in 8.5 hours and has a surface temperature of **5,119°F (2,826°C)**—hot enough to melt iron!

## Red-hot world

# LARGEST EXOPLANETS
## (TIMES EARTH)

1. **PZ Tel b—27.1**

2. **CT Cha b—24.64**

3. **HAT-P-32 b—22.81**

4. **WASP-17 b—22.3**

5. **KOI-368.01 b—20.5**

=5. **WASP-76—20.5**

7. **HAT-P-33 b—20.46**

8. **GQ Lup b—20.16**

9. **WASP-78 b—19.6**

10. **WASP-12 b—19.44**

## How many?

As many as one in five sunlike stars have an Earth-sized planet in the habitable Goldilocks zone (see page 11). These planets may have the right conditions for life to exist.

**20%**

## How exoplanets are discovered

Exoplanets are usually too dim to be seen directly, so **astronomers** look out for the effects they might have on other objects, such as the light from the stars they orbit or from other objects that are **farther away**.

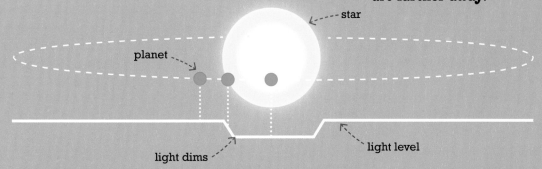

As the exoplanet travels **in front** of its star, it causes the star's light to **dim** slightly. Astronomers can use this method to calculate the **size** of the exoplanet.

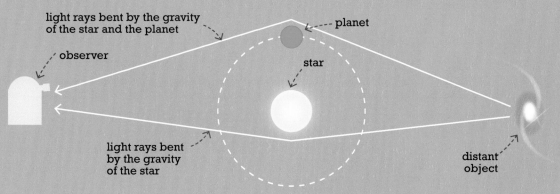

A star's **gravity** actually bends the light coming from a more distant object that's far **behind** it. If that star has a planet orbiting it, then the gravity of the planet will cause the light to bend **even more**, distorting the image of the distant object.

23

# STAR LIGHT, STAR BRIGHT

The sun is one of billions of stars that form our galaxy, which is called the Milky Way. This chart shows the 10 stars and star systems that are closest to us and their distance in light-years (ly).

## 9 Epsilon Eridani

This orange dwarf star has a large, Jupiter-sized planet orbiting it.

**10.52 ly**

15 light-years

10 light-years

5 light-years

## 4 Lalande 21185

Visible with the help of binoculars, this small red star is up to 10 billion years old.

**8.29 ly**

## 3 Wolf 359

This very dim red star was first seen in 1916.

**7.78 ly**

## Dense stars

Neutron stars are so dense that a teaspoonful of their matter would have a mass of **1.1 billion tons** (1 billion metric tons)—

equivalent to more than **1,500** fully loaded supertankers.

## 5 Sirius

This system contains two stars, Sirius A and Sirius B. Sirius A is the brightest star in our night sky.

**8.58 ly**

## 1 Alpha Centauri

This system is made up of three stars, the closest of which is called Proxima Centauri.

**4.24-4.37 ly**

## What is a light-year?

This is the distance light travels in one year. Light travels at 186,000 miles (300,000 km) a second (about 7.5 times around Earth).

**7.5 times**

That's equivalent to **5,878,499,811,103 miles (9,460,528,000 km) in a whole year!**

## 8 Ross 248

This is a single, small, dim red star.

### 10.32 ly

## Types of star

Astronomers classify stars in spectral types, depending on their color, makeup, and the temperature at which they burn. Each type is given a letter.

**O** — O stars are blue and have a temperature of up to 90,000°F (50,000°C).

**B** — B stars are blue-white stars and have a temperature of up to 50,000°F (28,000°C).

**A** — A stars are white and have a temperature of up to 18,000°F (10,000°C).

**F** — F stars are pale yellow and have a temperature of up to 13,500°F (7,500°C).

**G** — G stars, such as our sun, are yellow and have a temperature of up to 10,800°F (6,000°C).

**K** — K stars are orange and have a temperature of up to 8,900°F (4,900°C).

**M** — M stars are red and have a temperature of up to 6,300°F (3,500°C).

## 2 Barnard's Star

This small star is very dim and is not visible to the naked eye from Earth.

### 5.96 ly

## 6 Luyten 726

This system is made up of two small red stars that are slowly orbiting each other.

### 8–8.73 ly

## 7 Ross 154

This is a single red star.

### 9.68 ly

## 10 Lacaille 9352

Even though this is a red star, it is quite bright and can be seen using binoculars.

### 10.74 ly

# INTO SPACE

Humans have been exploring space for over 50 years, using robots or sending people into space. Launched in 1977, the spacecraft *Voyager 1* has now traveled over 11.8 billion miles (19 billion km)—farther than any other human-made object.

## Distance traveled by extraterrestrial rovers

Robot rovers have been extremely useful in exploring other bodies in the solar system. Many have lasted well beyond their scheduled missions, sending back vital information.

**Sojourner** (Mars)—0.06 miles (0.1 km)
This small rover was active on the Martian surface from July to September 1997.

**Spirit** (Mars)—4.8 miles (7.7 km)
This rover was active from 2004 until it became stuck in the Martian soil and lost contact in 2010.

**Curiosity** (Mars)—5.3 miles (8.6 km)
Landing on Mars in 2012, *Curiosity* is about the size of a small car.

**Lunokhod 1** (moon)—6.5 miles (10.5 km)
This Soviet craft was the first robot rover to explore another object in the solar system. This rover operated from November 1970 to September 1971.

### Eugene Cernan
drove Lunar Roving Vehicle in the Apollo 17 mission up to 11 miles (18 km) per hour, setting a speed record for extraterrestrial rovers.

## Moon rock

Between 1969 and 1972, the Apollo missions brought back **842 pounds (382 kg)** of lunar rock samples—more than the weight of **five people**.

# LONGEST HUMAN SPACEFLIGHTS

1. **Valeri Polyakov (Russia), 437.7 days (1994–1995)**

2. Sergei Avdeyev (Russia), 379.6 days (1998–1999)

3. **Vladimir Titov and Musa Manarov (USSR), 365.0 days (1987–1988)**

4. Yuri Romanenko (USSR), 326.5 days (1987)

5. **Sergei Krikalev (USSR/Russia), 311.8 days (1991–1992)**

6. Valeri Polyakov (USSR), 240.9 days (1988–1989)

7. **Leonid Kizim, Vladimir Solovyov, Oleg Atkov (USSR), 237.0 days (1984)**

8. Mikhail Tyurin, Michael López-Alegría (Russia, United States), 215.4 days (2006–2007)

9. **Anatoli Berezovoy, Valentin Lebedev (USSR), 211.4 days (1982)**

10. Talgat Musabayev, Nikolai Budarin (Russia), 207.5 days (1998)

## Animals in Space

Animals sent into space include dogs, cats, chimpanzees, monkeys, spiders, frogs, fish, crickets, and ants.

Tiny creatures called tardigrades (water bears) were even exposed to the freezing cold (**−458°F, or −272°C**) of space for 10 days and **survived!**

**Apollo 16 Lunar Roving Vehicle mission (moon)— 16.8 miles (27.1 km)**
Astronauts John Young and Charles Duke drove this rover around the moon in 1972.

**Apollo 15 Lunar Roving Vehicle mission (moon)— 17.3 miles (27.8 km)**
David Scott and James Irwin used this rover during their three-day stay on the moon in 1971.

**Apollo 17 Lunar Roving Vehicle mission (moon)— 22.2 miles (35.7 km)**
The last Apollo mission rover was driven by Eugene Cernan and Harrison Schmitt in 1972.

*Lunokhod 2* (moon)—24 miles (39 km)
This Soviet lunar rover was active from January to May 1973.

*Opportunity* (Mars)— 25 miles (40.2 km)
Identical to *Spirit*, this rover has remained active for more than 11 years.

## Food in space

Astronauts' food is precooked or processed so that it does not require refrigeration. Astronauts have 3.7 pounds (1.7 kg) of food to eat a day—the same weight as...

**...four cans of soup.**

# SIZE OF THE UNIVERSE

Space is enormous, which is why distances between stars and galaxies are measured in light-years. These images show some of the biggest astronomical bodies in the solar system, our galaxy, and beyond.

**1** ### Supercluster
These are some of the largest structures in the universe. The Virgo Supercluster is made up of more than 100 groups of galaxies, called clusters.

**110 million ly**

**2** ### Galaxy cluster
Galaxies join together to form clusters. The Virgo Cluster contains up to 2,000 galaxies.

**5 million ly**

**3** ### Galaxy
Stars join together to create galaxies. They can vary greatly in size and shape, but the galaxy NGC 6872 is one of the biggest and contains up to 2 trillion stars.

**522,000 ly**

## Star cluster

**4** Within galaxies, stars move about in groups called clusters. One of the biggest in our galaxy is a globular cluster called Omega Centauri.

**230 ly**

## Star

**5** One of the largest stars in our galaxy is VY Canis Majoris. It is more than 2,000 times the size of our sun.

**870 million miles (1.4 billion km)**

## Planet

**6** Jupiter is the largest planet in the solar system. It is a huge ball of gas with a solid core.

**88,846 miles (142,984 km)**

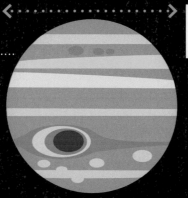

## Dwarf planet

**7** Ceres is one of the largest dwarf planets in the solar system. It orbits the sun in an area called the asteroid belt.

**590 miles (950 km)**

## Moon

**8** Moons are natural satellites that orbit around planets. The largest in the solar system is Ganymede.

**3,273 miles (5,268 km)**

## Asteroid

**9** The asteroid belt lies between Mars and Jupiter and contains millions of rocks. The largest of these asteroids is Pallas.

**339 miles (545 km)**

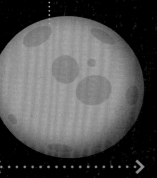

## Comet

**10** A comet's nucleus is a dirty snowball of ice and dust. Comet Hale-Bopp has the largest known nucleus.

**62 miles (100 km)**

# GLOSSARY

**acid rain**
rain with a high concentration of harmful, poisonous chemicals that can cause the rain to act like an acid, eroding things it lands on

**asteroid**
a large rock that orbits the sun. Asteroids are smaller than planets and are usually irregularly shaped, rather than spherical.

**axial tilt**
the amount by which a planet is tilted on its axis—the imaginary line running vertically through its center

**carbon dioxide**
a colorless, odorless gas present in the atmosphere. Animals, including humans, breathe in oxygen and breathe out carbon dioxide. Plants absorb carbon dioxide during photosynthesis.

**comet**
a small body made of ice and dust that travels in a long, stretched-out orbit around the sun. Comets heat up and begin to break apart near the sun, forming long tails of dust and gas.

**desert**
an area of Earth that receives very little rainfall and supports little or no vegetation. Deserts can be hot or cold.

**diameter**
the width of a circle or a sphere measured through its center point

**dwarf planet**
a body in the solar system that is spherically shaped, but not large enough to be considered a true planet

**exoplanet**
a planet that orbits a star outside of the solar system

**globular cluster**
a large, dense ball of stars that orbits around the center of a galaxy

**light-year**
a unit of measurement equal to the distance light travels in a year: around 6 trillion miles (9.6 trillion km)

**mass**
the amount of matter in a body or bodies

**orbit**
the path a body takes as it travels around another body, such as the moon traveling around Earth, or Earth traveling around the sun

**oxygen**
a colorless, odorless gas that makes up about 20 percent of Earth's atmosphere

**photosynthesis**
the process by which plants use the energy from sunlight to convert carbon dioxide and water from the ground into food and produce oxygen as a waste product

**rain shadow**
a region on one side of a mountainous area that remains dry because the mountains prevent the rain from reaching it

**rover**
a vehicle used to explore the surface of another planet or body. A rover can be manned or unmanned.

**shooting star**
a streak of light across the night sky, usually formed when a small piece of rock from an asteroid or a comet burns up in Earth's atmosphere

**solar system**
the sun plus all the objects that orbit it, including planets, dwarf planets, asteroids, and comets

**tectonic plates**
the giant pieces of rock that make up Earth's crust

**volume**
the amount of physical space taken up by a solid body, a liquid, or a gas.

**white dwarf**
a small, hot star formed when a larger star collapses in on itself toward the end of its life

# WEBSITES

◀ • • • • • • • • • • • • • • • • • • • • • • • • • • • • ▶

**Cool Infographics**
http://www.coolinfographics.com
These infographics and data visualizations are from other online resources, magazines, and newspapers.

**Daily Infographics**
http://www.dailyinfographic.com
This comprehensive collection of infographics on an enormous range of topics is updated every day.

**Data Visualization Encyclopedia**
http://www.visualinformation.info
This website contains a host of infographic material on subjects as diverse as natural history, science, sports, and computer games.

**Guinness World Records**
http://www.guinnessworldrecords.com
This website is for all things record-breaking. It is packed with thousands of world records and facts.

**NASA Kids' Club**
http://www.nasa.gov/audience/forkids /kidsclub/flash/
Lots of facts, games, images, and videos are available from NASA.

**Smithsonian Encyclopedia**
http://www.si.edu/Encyclopedia/
The Smithsonian's online encyclopedia is a great resource for facts about Earth and space.

# INDEX

**First American edition published in 2016 by Lerner Publishing Group, Inc.**

Copyright © 2015 by Wayland
published by arrangement with Wayland

Hungry Tomato™ is a trademark of Lerner Publishing Group, Inc.

Hungry Tomato™
A division of Lerner Publishing Group, Inc.
241 First Avenue North
Minneapolis, MN 55401 USA

For reading levels and more information, look up this title at www.lernerbooks.com.

Main body text set in Rockwell Std. Typeface provided by Monotype.

**Library of Congress Cataloging-in-Publication Data**

Richards, Jon, 1970– author.
  Record-breaking Earth & space facts / by Jon Richards and Ed Simkins.
    pages cm. — (Infographic top 10s)
  Audience: Ages 9–12
  Audience: Grades 4 to 6
  Includes bibliographical references and index.
  ISBN 978-1-4677-8595-2 (lb : alk. paper)
  ISBN 978-1-4677-9381-0 (pb : alk. paper)
  ISBN 978-1-4677-8646-1 (eb pdf)
  1. Earth (Planet)—Miscellanea—Juvenile literature. 2. Solar system—Miscellanea—Juvenile literature. 3. Children's questions and answers. I. Simkins, Ed, author. II. Title. III. Title: Record-breaking Earth and space facts.
  QB631.4.R48 2016
  525—dc23                                    2015002514

Manufactured in the United States of America
1 – BP – 7/15/15